Beautiful America's
Salem
Oregon

Beautiful America's
Salem
Oregon

Text by Elaine K. Sanchez
Photography by Ron Cooper

Beautiful America Publishing Company

Front cover: The city with Mt. Jefferson in the distance
Opposite title page: The State Capitol, with cherry blossoms

Published by
Beautiful America Publishing Company
P.O. Box 244
Woodburn, OR 97071

Library of Congress Catalog Number 2009033957

ISBN 978-0-89802-865-2
ISBN 978-0-89802-864-5 (paperback)

Copyright 2009 by Beautiful America Publishing Company ©

All Rights Reserved
No portion of this book is to be reproduced
in any form, including electronic media
without written permission from the publisher.

Printed in Korea

Contents

Introduction 8

Welcome to Salem 13

Medical 16

Education 18

Agriculture 22

Wine Country 23

Attractions 23

Parks & Family Attractions 37

Events 66

About the Author 78

About the Photographer 79

Salem from the air showing many of its attractions

Riverfront Park, the Riverfront Carousel, Willamette Queen Sternwheeler and Union Street Railroad Pedestrian Bridge

The Golden Pioneer and the First United Methodist Church steeple, two Salem landmarks

Introduction

When I was asked to write this book, I accepted immediately. Although my husband and I are transplants and have only lived here since 1998, we now consider Salem our "home town."

It's exciting to be in a position to share some of the things that make this city such a wonderful place to work, live, and play. But I've puzzled over where to begin. When describing Salem, do you start with the beauty? The history? The culture? There were so many things to consider, that I decided to enlist the help of some friends.

In a totally random and unscientific survey, I asked people to describe Salem in one word. Many words were brought up repeatedly, including: opportunity, diverse, and evolving. But the two words most frequently mentioned were community, and not surprisingly, location, location, location.

Situated in the middle of the verdant Willamette Valley, 47 miles south of Portland, and 64 miles north of Eugene, Salem is smack in the center of Oregon farm and wine country. (There are more than 500,000 acres of farmland and 30 wineries in Marion and Polk counties alone.) We are close to the snow-capped Cascade Mountains, and just slightly more than an hour's drive from the Pacific Ocean. So whether you are into wine tasting, hiking, skiing, golfing, canoeing, fly fishing, deep-sea fishing, whale watching, or simply lounging on the beach, recreational opportunities abound in and around Salem.

The Indian name for the area was Chemeketa, meaning "meeting or resting place." When the plats for the city were filed in 1850-51, the city was named Salem, after the Hebrew word Shalom, which means peace.

It is the state capital of Oregon, the county seat of Marion County, and the state's second-largest city with a population of approximately 160,000. The climate is temperate. It rarely gets above 80 in the summer and seldom dips below 30 in the winter. People may try to tell you that it rains all of the time in Oregon, but that simply is not true. Salem gets an average of 39 inches of annual rainfall, most of which falls November through March. There are actually about 216 rainless days each year. And if you're planning a wedding or an outdoor picnic, you might want to do it on July 12th, because as long as people have been keeping weather records, it has only rained twice in Salem on that date.

There are four distinct seasons. Spring, which starts mid-March and goes through May, is absolutely spectacular. The colors and varieties of the flowering bushes and trees are simply outrageous.

Summer is warm and sunny. The days are long, humidity is low, and bugs are scarce. Farmers and gardeners enjoy 204 glorious days in the average growing season.

Fall is fantastic. One October when my daughter and I were on a hike in the Cascades, I said, "These colors are so amazing, I just don't know how to describe them." After a few minutes, she replied, "The combination of reds, oranges, golds, and greens sort of reminds me of a 1970's psychedelic hippie van." (I couldn't disagree; but I remember the 1970's, and I promise, these colors are much more beautiful in nature than they ever were on a couch, a car, or a shag carpet.)

Winter is wet. There's no denying that we go through a long stretch of short, gray, soggy days from November through March. The upside is that lawns are green even in the middle of winter, and most years you can get by without owning a snow shovel or an ice scraper.

In addition to the beauty and the area's tremendous natural resources, Salem is a city comprised of a number of vibrant communities in the areas of government, business, agriculture, education, art, theater, music, history, recreation, and social services.

The common factors that have led to the success and growth of these various communities are a number of visionary leaders, a capable workforce, and leagues of volunteers who continually donate their talent, time, and money to create, preserve, and maintain a wide range of facilities and programs.

One of the greatest things about Salem is how easy it is to become a part of the community. You don't have to be a titan of industry, have an impressive family name, or even have a lot of money. You just have to show up. If you are willing to share your expertise and donate your time, you can get involved, develop a network of friends, and make a difference in a very short period of time.

Throughout the pages of this book you will read about a number of venues totally unique to Salem. Many historic sites, such as the Elsinore Theatre, Bush House, Mission Mill Museum, and Deepwood Estate have been saved, restored, and preserved by individuals who simply refused to let the historic people, stories, and events that made this community special fall into the forgotten past.

There are also a number of relatively new attractions, such as Salem's Riverfront Carousel, A.C. Gilbert's Discovery Village, the Eco-Earth Globe, and the Ray and Joan KROC Corps Community Center, that came about because someone had an idea and a passion for creating something that would entertain, inspire, and enhance the lives of the community's children and their families.

If you are a visitor, you will discover that there is much to see and do in Salem. And if you are lucky enough to live here, you already know that housing is affordable, traffic is manageable, and health care is excellent.

This is a community that has preserved its past by designating a number of areas as Historic Districts, while at the same time going boldly into the future by creating several hundred acres of shovel-ready

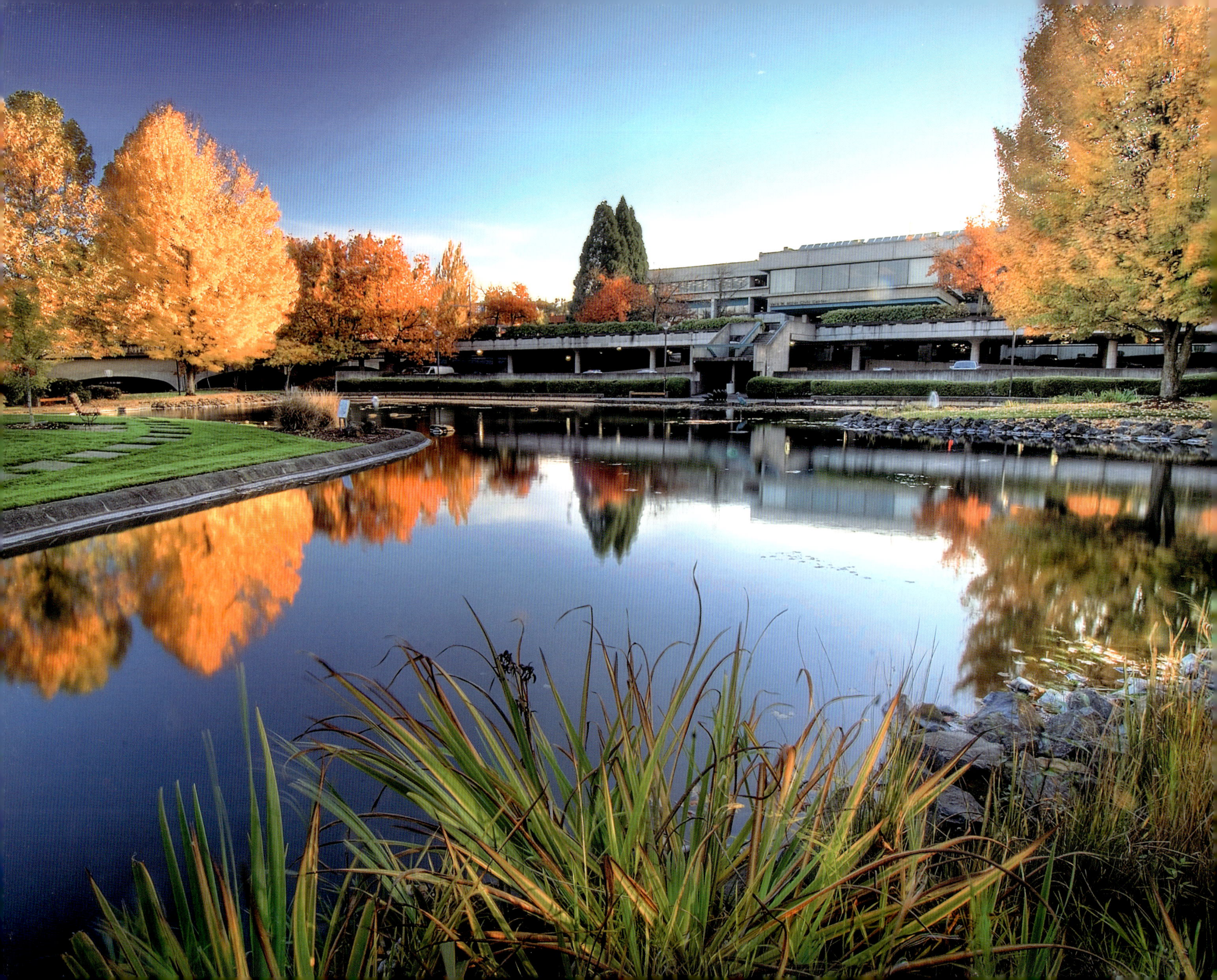

Pringle Park in full bloom

Opposite: Civic Center on a crisp fall day

industrial sites of varying sizes, including the Mill Creek Corporate Center and Salem's Renewable Energy and Technology Center. Salem's livability and quality workforce has attracted international companies such as SANYO Solar of Oregon LLC, Garmin AT, Yamasa Soy Sauce, and IMEX to locate here, thereby providing progressive and diverse employment opportunities.

There is a lovely new conference center and a number of recently constructed avant-garde business/residential buildings that are bringing new energy and vitality to an already active downtown. And as this book is being written, residents are eagerly watching the wrecking ball, bulldozers, and front end loaders demolish the old Boise Cascade plant located adjacent to Riverfront Park. An exciting new development featuring restaurants, retail shops, offices, and condominiums will take its place. This new complex will be within walking distance of everything downtown and will feature stunning views of water, trees, and the hills of west Salem.

Salem is business friendly, and at the same time a place where people appreciate and protect the environment. Many of the new buildings around town are "Green." Salem's Pringle Creek LLC Sustainable Housing Development won the National Home Builders Innovative Project of the Year in 2007. Several area wineries practice sustainable agriculture. Organic fruits and vegetables are readily available at the Wednesday and Saturday Farmer's Market. The tap water, which originates high in the Cascades, is as sweet, clean, and pure as anything you can buy in a bottle; and our recycle bins are significantly larger than our garbage cans.

Garten Services, a nonprofit organization serving people with developmental disabilities and long-term mental illnesses, has developed a project called Zero Waste Events. It's a new way of handling discarded items from festivals, trade shows, and other large-scale gatherings. Instead of thinking of the waste as garbage, these articles get recycled, which provides jobs and raw material for new products.

The list of Salem's attributes is long. There are three incredibly beautiful and challenging golf courses – one public, two private. There's a new $6 million "Center 50+" that offers recreational, educational, and social opportunities for seniors. There's an outstanding library close to downtown and a branch library in west Salem. Together they lend out 1.3 million items annually. There is also great shopping and numerous interesting restaurants featuring a wide array of cuisine and price points.

But the thing I appreciate most is the people. Roots run deep here. Kids grow up and stay. Neighbors look out for each other, businesses support one another, and the success of one is celebrated by many. It's a great place to visit -- and an even better place to live.

Welcome to Salem!

Downtown Salem

When most cities across the country started building huge mall complexes in the suburbs, Salem took a different approach and built its mall right in the heart of downtown. Salem Center is a five-block complex that offers over 80 specialty shops all connected by a series of sky bridges that are linked to four major department stores: Nordstrom, J.C. Penney, Kohl's, and Macy's.

The streets surrounding the Salem Center are lined with shops, boutiques, art galleries, restaurants, coffee shops, and bars. Each street is like its own little community and has a totally unique personality and charm.

A must-see shop on State Street is the Mary Lou Zeek Gallery. Don't be fooled by the size. Huge things come out of this tiny space. You will find exceptional quality art created by local, regional, and national artists. And there is always some kind of wonderful event being developed that allows artists to stretch their abilities and show their work. Whether it's the Door Show or the 100 Artists Show, you can be assured that the Mary Lou Zeek Gallery has something fabulous on the walls and in the works.

The Reed Opera House, on the corner of Liberty and Court streets, is another place you shouldn't miss. Built in 1869-70 by Cyrus Adams Reed, it was originally intended to house the State Library, Supreme Court, and the Oregon State Legislature. Following an election, the new administration had a change of heart, and Mr. Reed had to improvise. He redesigned the building to include seven shops, a hotel, and a 1,500-seat theater, which was quite ambitious considering Salem's entire population was just 1,139 in 1870! Liberty Street was unpaved and deeply rutted; and drinking, gambling, and fist fights were the primary entertainment after dark.

Today, the Reed Opera House is home to the Salem Repertory Theatre, a nonprofit organization that creates and presents professional theatrical events. There are a variety of shops where you can buy everything from designer clothing for your dog to furniture made by Amish Craftsmen. After you finish shopping you can have a bite to eat at one of the five eclectic restaurants.

The south end of downtown is anchored by the Salem Conference Center and the Phoenix Grand Hotel. Opened in 2005, this stunning structure offers a spacious 30,000 square feet of meeting space. The architects and designers accomplished their goal of developing a building that reflects the natural beauty and relaxed lifestyle of Oregon's Willamette Valley. You can be in a group of more than 1,000 people in the Willamette River Room and feel like you are in an intimate setting.

The Phoenix Grand Hotel

Salem's state-of-the-art Conference Center

Connected to the Conference Center is the beautiful Phoenix Grand Hotel. All 193 over-sized guest rooms and suites offer separate work and living areas and complimentary wireless high-speed Internet access. Some rooms have Jacuzzis and fireplaces. And to help guests unwind after a full day of attending a conference, conducting business, or sightseeing, there is an indoor pool, a fitness center, spa, and a full-service restaurant with an extensive wine bar and great happy-hour specials.

Living in the Center of it All -- 2009 was a big year for one of the newest and most exciting additions to Salem -- Downtown Living.

The Rivers Condominiums, on the west edge of downtown, is an exclusive development that offers a combination of retail space, live-work units, and 22 luxury condos with panoramic views of Riverfront Park, the Willamette River, and downtown Salem.

The Meridian, just south of Salem's Conference Center, and within easy walking distance of everything downtown, is a mixed-use six-story building. Offices and condos on the west side of the property overlook the Willamette River, while people on the east side get to enjoy the vistas of the Cascade mountain range.

295 Church, at the corner of Church and Trade streets, is another mixed-use project. There are five stories. The first two floors are commercial office space and home to the studios and offices of Salem's public-access television station, Capital Community Television (CCTV). The top three floors are divided into 27 residential-condominium units offering a variety of views including the Cascade Range and Pringle Park.

Medical

Salem Hospital

Salem Hospital is the leading regional medical center in the mid-Willamette Valley. For example in heart care, HealthGrades(R), an independent healthcare ratings organization, ranked Salem Hospital No. 1 in Oregon for overall heart services for 2009. Salem Hospital also has the busiest emergency department in the state of Oregon.

In April 2009 Salem Hospital opened its newest addition, a technologically advanced critical-care tower that was designed to accommodate foreseeable medical advances for the next 50 years. It offers an expanded emergency room, imaging department, surgery suites, and critical care for patients with heart problems and traumatic injuries.

Shopping paradise — Kelly James Photography

When you step into this new facility, you are immediately impressed with the attention to detail. Evidence-based design guided the planning of this healing environment for patients, families and staff starting with the music of a grand piano that greets visitors in the main lobby. A chapel welcomes people of all faiths with beechwood carvings representing many of the area's faith communities. The "Healing Art" collection, 50 plus original works by 21 Willamette Valley artists, features the colors and textures of the Pacific Northwest in natural landscapes.

Based on research that shows the importance of natural light, privacy, and the presence of loved ones, the new tower was designed so that each patient's private room has a large window with impressive views of Salem—from beautiful Bush Park, to the striking Capitol building, to the Cascade range. There are even couches that convert into beds so family members have a comfortable place to rest while staying with loved ones.

Education

Salem-Keizer School District

With nearly 40,000 students, the Salem-Keizer School District is the second-largest school district in the state. There are 45 elementary schools, 10 middle schools, 8 high schools, and 4 charter schools in the district. A poll shows the students are ethnically diverse, with a mix of Caucasian, Hispanic, multi-ethnic, Asian/Pacific Islander, African American and Native American.

The teachers and administrators strive to ensure that each student will have the essential knowledge and skills to compete in a changing and increasingly diverse world. On college entrance exams, Salem-Keizer students score above the national average.

In music programs, Salem-Keizer high schools excel. Having been awarded 10 Grammy Signature Schools awards, Salem-Keizer has won more Grammy Awards than any other school district in the United States.

Chemeketa Community College

Chemeketa Community College serves 64,000 students each year. It is the region's resource for accessible, quality education, technical training, workforce development, and business support. The main campus is located on the northeast side of Salem, with branch campuses in McMinnville, Dallas, and Woodburn.

Chemeketa offers Associate of Applied Science degrees in more than 40 professional-technical programs, as well as Associate of Arts, Oregon Transfer, and General Education degrees. It is well known for its nursing, fire science, graphic arts, and electronics programs.

Across town in west Salem, at the beautiful Northwest Viticulture Center, students can earn an Associate of Applied Science degree in Vineyard Management, Winemaking, and/or Wine Marketing. (Imagine taking college classes that include wine tasting as part of the curriculum.)

In 2009 Chemeketa opened its new Center for Business & Industry, which houses the Small Business Development Center and provides an excellent resource for workforce training and business development in the community.

Corban College & Graduate School

Corban College & Graduate School is a residential, independent Christian college established in 1935 offering undergraduate and graduate level degrees.

Students can choose from more than 50 majors and programs of study including professional, liberal arts, and ministries. Along with traditional and adult degree-completion programs at the undergraduate level, Corban offers post-baccalaureate teacher licensure and graduate degrees in education, business administration, and counseling.

Willamette University

Willamette University, established in 1842, was the first university in the West. It is actually older than the cities of Salem, Portland, Seattle, and Tacoma, and it has a long history of philanthropy. When Oregon was admitted to the Union in 1859, the University actually deeded the land to the new state for the construction of the Capitol building. Much of Salem's present downtown is built on former University land.

Willamette also has a long-established history of excellence in education. It is a top-tier private liberal arts university with a reputation for admitting the most talented, the highest achieving, and most promising students. After graduation, a large number of Willamette's graduates go on to prestigious graduate and professional schools, including Willamette's School of Education, College of Law, and the Atkinson School of Business Management.

Its Tokyo International University of America, pioneered in 1965, has provided more than 1,700 Japanese students the opportunity to participate in a one-year American Studies program. They study English,

Award-winning Salem Hospital — Steve Wanke Photography

Willamette University – oldest university in the West

sociology, politics, economics, intercultural management, literature, and history. In addition to becoming immersed in an American college experience, students also get involved in the Salem community through the Tomodachi (Friendship) Family Program as well as cultural and volunteer activities.

Willamette University is recognized nationally for its leadership in sustainability and commitment to social justice. Its motto, "Not unto ourselves alone are we born," encourages students to contribute to the greater good of the global community. Current students dedicate 60,000 plus hours a year to volunteer projects, and more than 270 Willamette alumni have joined the Peace Corps since its inception in 1961.

Students in the 2008 Princeton Review of the nation's best colleges described Willamette University as "academically rigorous," "intimate," and "seriously gorgeous." The campus, located across from Oregon's Capitol, offers the best of the Northwest – lovely open spaces interspersed with ancient trees, flowering bushes, and a peaceful stream.

Agriculture

The Willamette Valley, possibly the most diverse agriculture region on earth, is named for the river that runs through it. The Valley starts in Portland and stretches 150 miles to the Calapooya Mountains south of Eugene. Approximately 60 miles wide, it is bordered by the Cascade Mountains on the east and the Coast Range on the west.

Rich volcanic soil deposited from massive flood waters 10,000 years ago, along with abundant rainfall, sunny summer days, and moist, cool winds off the Pacific Ocean, provide an ideal growing climate for a wide variety of agricultural products.

More than 170 different crops, including fruits, berries, grapes, vegetables, nursery products, grains, Christmas trees, flowers, nuts, grasses and legume seeds are successfully grown here. In addition, farmers raise dairy, poultry, beef, and sheep.

Thanks to aggressive land-use laws, fertile farm ground has not been gobbled up by developers. A drive through Oregon farm country provides some of the most breath-taking vistas of this magnificently lush and fertile valley.

Wine Country

Wine making in Oregon is a relatively new industry. In the mid-sixties, three men from U.C. Davis in California believed that Oregon provided a perfect environment for growing cool-climate varieties. Despite being told it was impossible to grow wine grapes in Oregon, they planted the first Pinot Noir vines. They also planted small amounts of Pinot Gris, Chardonnay, and Riesling.

In 1979 when an Oregon Pinot Noir beat all of France's best labels to win top honors in the Gault-Millau French Wine Olympiad, the world took notice.

Currently there are approximately 12,000 acres of grapes under cultivation and more than 200 wineries producing wines of impeccable quality in the Willamette Valley.

Based in Salem, it is easy to pack a picnic, go for a leisurely drive in the country and spend the afternoon sampling wines from a few of the many, many wineries with tasting rooms. You can find them by following highway directional signs, but it's a lot more efficient to get a free wine-tour guide from Travel Salem, or rent a pre-programmed GPS with wine-tours and a variety of other tours for easy use. You could also book a tour with a knowledgeable guide that will take you to a variety of wineries, large and small, and in addition to sampling a variety of wines, you could also take a tour and learn how the wine is made.

Attractions

Oregon State Capitol

The beautiful white marble Art Deco building with the Oregon Pioneer (gold man) on top, is Oregon's third capitol. The first one burned in 1855, the second one in 1935. The current capitol was constructed from 1936 to 1938, during the Great Depression with financial help from the federal government Public Works Administration.

When you walk into the spacious rotunda, you just have to stand for a minute or two to take it all in. It is 106 feet from the large bronze replica of the Oregon State Seal on the floor to the thirty-three stars painted on the ceiling of the dome, which represent Oregon becoming the thirty-third state in the Union.

There are magnificent examples of Depression-era art in the murals, including four that represent important events in Oregon's history: Captain Robert Gray at the mouth of the Columbia River in 1792; Lewis and Clark on their way to the Pacific in 1805; the first women to cross the continent by covered wagon in 1836; and the first wagon train migration in 1843.

Newly restored Elsinore Theatre lobby

Historic Deepwood Estate

The golden pioneer on the top of the dome was built in New Jersey and then shipped to Oregon via the Panama Canal in 1938. It traveled by rail to Salem. He stands 23 feel tall, weighs 8.5 tons, and is covered in 23K gold leaf. He has a beard, and according to the artist, he holds an axe in one hand and a wagon cover in the other to use as a shelter. He stands as a beacon of the pioneering spirit of Oregonians, and he shines even at night due to the solar panels on the Capitol's rooftop.

Salem's Capitol building houses the state legislature, the offices of the governor, secretary of state, and the state treasurer. And for a few weeks each March, thousands of people come to the Capitol Mall to enjoy the magnificent cherry trees in bloom. Some think they rival the beauty of the cherry trees in Washington D.C. You might have to climb the 121 steps from the fourth floor to the observation deck to decide for yourself.

The Historic Elsinore Theatre

There may be no better example of community involvement than The Historic Elsinore Theatre. Built on a former livery stable site, and designed to resemble the castle in *Hamlet*, Shakespeare's greatest drama, the Elsinore first opened its doors to the public on May 28, 1926.

It quickly became recognized as the finest theater between Portland and San Francisco. For several years audiences enjoyed silent movies and live vaudeville performances twice a week. In 1929 it was converted to accommodate the newest technological advance in entertainment – talking movies.

Every Thursday during the 1930's talented young people would line up at the Elsinore to audition for Zollie's Mickey Mouse Club Matinee. The best singers, dancers, and musicians would be selected to perform the following Saturday. Created and hosted by teenage impresario Zollie Volchok, the show featured a group of "regulars," including the talented young trumpeter, Doc Severinsen.

Over the course of the next four decades, the Elsinore was sold a number of times, and the forces of time, nature, and audience abuse took their toll. By the late 1970's the theatre once billed as "The Showplace of the Willamette Valley" had lost its appeal even as a second-run, discount movie house.

In 1980 plans were being made to demolish the Elsinore and replace it with a parking lot. A group of concerned citizens, appalled at the thought of losing this local, historical treasure, formed a grassroots organization called the "Save the Elsinore Committee."

Through plain stubborn effort, this group obtained a number of grants and recruited a committed cadre of volunteers and finally managed to purchase the theatre and perform some badly needed repairs. In 1994 the Elsinore was put on the National Register of Historic Places.

In February 2000, when Gregory Peck gave the final performance of his career on the Historic Elsinore Theatre stage he said, "I just wanted to say you have to do great things with a theatre like this. I am so impressed . . . It's quite possibly the outstanding venue on our tour. I am most enthusiastic about the possibilities of this theatre and I hope you will lend your strongest support. . ."

The next year, on the Elsinore's 75th anniversary, a group of prominent local individuals stepped forward to champion the Return to Grandeur Campaign. The board of directors resolved to keep the theatre operating and fiscally sound, while at the same time rebuilding its infrastructure, repairing its damage, and returning it to its original glory.

It took three years and $3.2 million in grants and donations to rebuild and restore this fabulous structure. Thanks to the persistence of a number of dedicated volunteers who stepped forward at different times to take on the monumental and sometimes unpopular challenges of saving the theatre, renovating it, funding it, and managing it, The Elsinore has survived time, weather, owner neglect, and public apathy.

It now hosts an average of 140 events a year, including top national performances, regional talent, films, private parties, and weddings.

Historic Deepwood Estate

The Victorian era is alive and well on the four-acre grounds of the Historic Deepwood Estate, located next to Bush Park, just a few blocks south of downtown Salem. At Deepwood you can take a class to learn how to crochet, attend a "Fanciful Fashion Tea," and partake in a wine and food festival. You can also tour the home, admire the elegant, manicured gardens, and then enjoy a bit of solitude with a shady stroll on the Rita Steiner Nature Trail.

The Queen Anne Victorian home was completed in 1894 at a cost of $15,000 when the average home in Salem cost $1,000. In 2002 *Sunset Magazine* named it as one of the four "Best Historic Homes" in its "Best of the West" section. The home is magnificently maintained, including the stained glass windows which were designed by the famed Povey Brothers of Portland.

The English-style gardens were commissioned by the home's third owner in 1929 and designed by Elizabeth Lord and Edith Schryver, the Northwest's first professionally trained female landscape architects. Their design reflects the concept of garden "rooms."

The museum is operated by the Friends of Deepwood, a nonprofit organization. It's fun to take a tour and learn about the history of the home and the people who lived in it. And it's a perfect place to visit with a notebook if you'd like to take notes on how to create your own boxwood or English tea house garden, or if you would like to see how to make a graceful transition from a manicured garden into a wild, natural area.

Mission Mill Museum — Magic at the Mill

The Bush House with wisteria in full bloom

Mission Mill Museum

If anyone in your family moved to Oregon in the mid-1800's, it might have been due to the efforts of a missionary by the name of Jason Lee. And if you had relatives who prospected for gold in Alaska in the early 1900's or fought in World War I or World War II, it is possible that they slept under a blanket, wore a heavy mackinaw jacket or a military uniform made from the wool processed at the Thomas Kay Woolen Mill in Salem.

So how are the stories of Jason Lee, the Missionary and Thomas Lister Kay, the Industrialist linked? It all began in 1833 in Boston. Jason Lee was ordained as Missionary to the Indians by the Methodist Church. Along with four other missionaries, Jason Lee traveled across the country on horseback with a group of fur traders (the only white people in the Oregon Territory at the time.) They arrived in 1834.

Mr. Lee's success at converting Indians to Christianity was minimal. However, he played a major role in attracting settlers through civilizing the territory. His work was instrumental in establishing schools and churches along with large-scale industry and agriculture.

So, thanks to Jason Lee, when twenty-year-old Thomas Kay arrived from England in 1857, the sheep-growing industry was already well established. Mr. Kay got a job as a loom boss. In 1889 he founded his own woolen mill.

When the mill closed in 1962, people in the community recognized the historic value of the property and made the decision to preserve it for future generations. In 1964 they established a private, nonprofit organization, and purchased the Mill. In addition to preserving the buildings on the site, they moved and restored some of the historic buildings from Jason Lee's Mission sites, and created a venue that has earned the designation of an American Treasure by the National Park Service.

Mission Mill is the only woolen mill museum west of Missouri and it has one of the few water-powered turbines in the Pacific Northwest that still generates electricity from a millrace.

The mission houses, parsonage, and church were built in the 1840s and 1850s, and are thought to be the oldest remaining frame houses in the Pacific Northwest. Classes for the Indian Manual Training School may have been conducted in the Parsonage while the school was being built. That school evolved into the Oregon Institute and eventually became Willamette University.

Mission Mill is open year round for tours, meetings, and shopping, and every Christmas it is lit up with thousands of holiday lights. Families delight in artisan demonstrations, musical performances, and children's activities.

You might be surprised to learn that the Pendleton Woolen Mills is still owned and operated by Thomas Kay's descendants. So if you have ever had the pleasure of curling up under an intricately designed Pendleton blanket or wearing one of their wonderful wool garments, then you have experienced a bit of a connection to Salem's history.

Bush House Museum

Many cities can identify a family that amassed a great deal of wealth and power and then did something good for the community in return. The name "Bush" is significant in Salem's history. Asahel Bush II founded the Ladd and Bush Bank and the *Oregon Statesman* newspaper - now the *Statesman Journal*. Upon his death in 1913, his estate was the largest in Oregon's inheritance-tax history.

His Victorian Italianate-style home, built in 1877, which sits on the north end of Bush Park, was the focal point of his huge estate. It included a large barn, a greenhouse, and acres of open cattle pastures. Although he had great wealth, he also suffered great tragedy. His beautiful wife died at a young age and left him with four children.

Upon Mr. Bush's death, the home and property passed on to his children. His second daughter "Aunt Sally" served as the hostess of the house for thirty years. When she died the home went to her brother A.N. Bush who arranged for the house and grounds to go to the City of Salem upon his death.

The home is now an historic house museum. It is a wonderful example of the time period, as many of the furnishings, including the wallpaper are original. The home is lovingly preserved by members of the Bush House Auxiliary.

Bush Barn Art Center

Once home to the Bush family's farm equipment, the Bush Barn was used as the park's maintenance facility until a fire destroyed the building in 1963. The Salem Art Association got permission to rebuild the structure and turn it into a gallery. Donations from the public along with the insurance settlement provided the funds to build the Bush Barn, which is now owned by the City and managed by the Art Association. The center hosts two contemporary exhibition galleries, a consignment gallery, and the offices of the Salem Art Association.

In the A.N. Bush Gallery you will find major exhibitions of regional, national and international artists. The Focus Gallery showcases contemporary work by local artists.

Bush House Museum amid the lush and vivid Bush's Pasture Park

The Camas Gallery features juried arts and crafts from more than 150 different Pacific Northwest artists. This is a great place to buy gifts for yourself or for loved ones. When you purchase any of the fabulous jewelry, glass, pottery, paintings, and textiles, the artist receives 60 percent and 40 percent goes to support the Art Association's education and exhibition programs. Everybody wins!

Hallie Ford Museum of Art

Named for a philanthropist who worked tirelessly to benefit education and the arts in Oregon, the Hallie Ford Museum of Art opened in 1998. The museum showcases Willamette University's collection of European, Asian, and Native American art. It supports the liberal arts curriculum for Willamette students and also serves as a cultural resource for the City of Salem. In addition to its permanent exhibit, the Hallie Ford Museum is gaining recognition for its exciting visiting collections featuring regional artists and craftspeople.

Pentacle Theatre

A 189-seat country playhouse, situated in a stand of Oregon Oaks and Douglas Firs, the Pentacle Theatre, a nonprofit community theater company, has presented top-quality productions for more than 55 years. They offer eight shows annually featuring a great combination of comedies, dramas, and musicals. The quality of the performances is impressive and ticket prices are more than reasonable.

Spirit Mountain Casino and Lodge

The history of the Confederated Tribes of Grand Ronde in Western Oregon goes back hundreds of years. Their respect for nature and cultural heritage is reflected in the architecture and design of the Spirit Mountain Casino and Lodge, one of Oregon's most popular tourist destinations.

Approximately 25 miles west of Salem, it is an enjoyable drive through gorgeous rolling hills of farm land and grape vineyards. And if you'd prefer to look at the scenery rather than pay attention to the road, you can take a Casino shuttle.

With 90,000 square feet of casino gaming, you can have fun playing everything from slot machines to roulette, bingo, poker, and a wide variety of other games.

If you're hungry when you arrive, you can have a quick bite at a gaming table, enjoy a casual meal in a cafe, partake in a bountiful buffet, or opt for Northwest-inspired cuisine accompanied by fine Oregon wines and live entertainment in an elegant dining room.

Spirit Mountain Casino, west of Salem

Ray and Joan Kroc Corps Community Center (opened September 2009)

There are three bars: a sports bar with 17 HD television screens, a sophisticated rocking nightclub, and a comfy lounge where you can hang back and listen to free live entertainment ranging from country to rock.

If you go to Spirit Mountain to enjoy a performance by a world-class entertainer, you could stay in one of the 254 lodge rooms that range from deluxe to decadent. Whether you like to gamble, eat, drink, dance, or just relax, it's all about fun in Grand Ronde, where the game never ends.

The Oregon Garden

First opened to the public in 2001, The Oregon Garden is a fabulous 80-acre botanical garden in Silverton, featuring more than 20 specialty gardens, including a Conifer Garden, a Northwest Garden, a Pet-Friendly Garden and a 25-acre native White Oak grove, that includes a 100-foot tall, 400 year-old Signature Oak that has been designated one of Oregon's "Heritage Trees." The Garden is also home to the Gordon House, the only house in Oregon designed by the legendary architect, Frank Lloyd Wright. You can enjoy a relaxed and informative tram ride through The Garden, or spend all the time you wish just wandering among the incredible displays of flowers, bushes, grasses, waterfalls, quiet ponds, and fountains. And don't forget to visit The Oregon Garden Gift Shop and Café.

Kids love the "weird plants" in the Children's Garden, and they have a great time digging for dinosaur bones, exploring a "jungle" from the vantage of a tree house, and climbing in and around a genuine Hobbit House.

In the fall of 2008, the addition of a 103-room boutique hotel made The Oregon Garden a destination resort. So if you appreciate the beauty of nature and also like being pampered at a spa, listening to music in a comfortable lounge, and dining on delicious Northwest-inspired cuisine, you might want to book a night's stay. Each room features luxurious garden-themed furnishings, a fireplace and private landscaped patio.

Silver Falls State Park

If you like nature, and you enjoy hiking, a trip to Silver Falls State Park is an absolute must! About a half-hour's drive southeast from Salem, this spectacular park is nestled in the lower elevation of the Cascade Mountains.

There are campsites, picnic areas, swimming holes, 25 miles of hiking trails and 14 miles of horse trails. But the take-your-breath-away-beautiful-not-to-be-missed hike is the Trail of Ten Falls/Canyon Trail. This seven-mile loop features 10 waterfalls. The trail actually takes you behind and beneath four of them. It is an absolute thrill to be cooled by the mist on a warm summer day as you stand behind South Falls and watch the water thunder past you as it falls 177 feet to Silver Creek.

If you are energetic, you can park at North Falls, follow the Canyon Trail to the lodge at South Falls, enjoy one of the best sandwiches in the entire world for a very reasonable price, and then follow the Rim trail back to your car. You will be amazed at the spectacular ancient Douglas fir, hemlock, and cedar trees towering above you, and the ferns, mosses, and wildflowers that grow along the trail.

Silver Falls also offers a spectacular location for meetings, small conferences, weddings, and family gatherings. Low-cost lodging is available in individual cabins and group lodges. Reasonably priced, delicious and filling meals are served in a dining hall situated under soaring trees. It is an exquisite experience you will want to do again and again.

Parks & Family Attractions

Bush's Pasture Park

Eighty-nine acres of rolling hills, open pastures, and natural spaces are all within a few minutes' walk of downtown Salem. In addition to the historic Bush House Museum and the Bush Barn Art Center, there are playgrounds, ball fields, tennis courts, picnic areas, walking paths, a soap box derby track, and the Willamette University state-of-the-art track and field complex.

There is also an outstanding collection of flowering trees, formal rose and flower gardens, an 1882 conservatory and a new Victorian-style gazebo ideally situated for outdoor weddings. A group of faithful volunteers, known as the Friends of Bush Gardens, help the City maintain the extensive gardens and conservatory.

And some day, if you are out for a stroll, you may observe a lady in a red hat pulling ivy and blackberries off of the slope that divides the upper and lower portions of the park. Her name is Sofia, and every year on January 27 (Mozart's birthday) she starts a new "concerto." During the first five years she cleared the tree wells around 687 of the park's ancient oaks. She started her sixth concerto in the winter of 2009. It is her intention to clear all of the bramble from the slope so that everyone can enjoy the lamb's tongue, trillium, Solomon seal, yellow viola, and camas lilies that bloom in the spring.

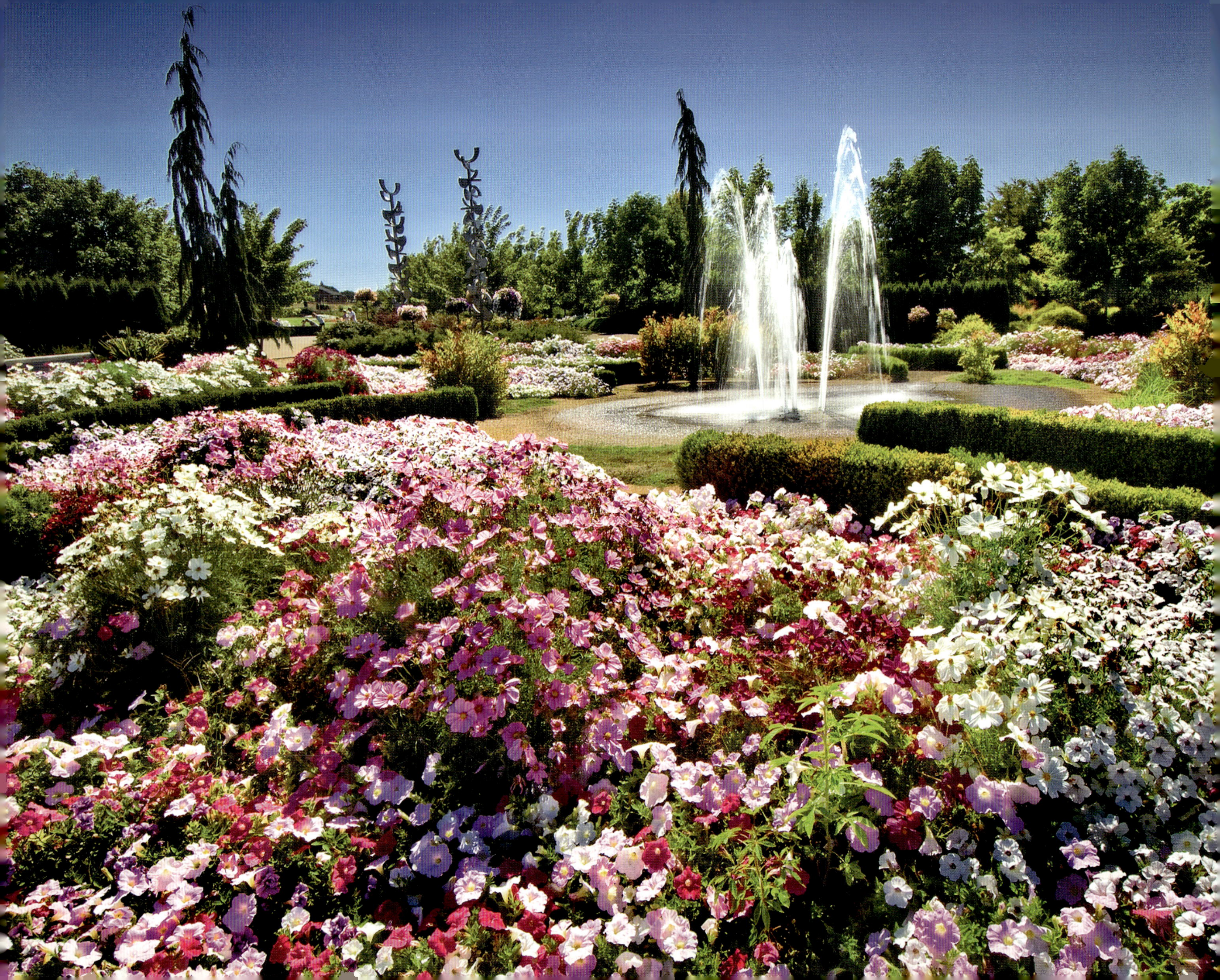

A must visit, Silver Falls State Park, south of Silverton

Opposite: Simply delightful – The Oregon Garden, Silverton

Minto-Brown Island Park

Early settlers, John Minto and Isaac "Whiskey" Brown (guess where he got the nickname) farmed on islands separated by the Willamette River. Minto's Island was on the east bank and Brown's Island was on the west bank. The floods of 1861 changed the river's course, and the area eventually became known as Minto-Brown Island.

In the early 1970's the City of Salem and Marion County purchased separate parcels of the site and combined them to create the amazing 900-acre Minto-Brown Island Park. It takes multiple trips through all four seasons to really appreciate all this park has to offer.

You can start your exploration by setting out on one of the many paved or mulched walking and biking trails that will take you along side the river and through different plots of farm ground where you might see crops such as corn, beans, potatoes, cabbage, wheat, pumpkins, and grass seed. You will pass through hazelnut orchards, see people fishing on the banks of sloughs, and in the late summer if you think you smell berry cobbler baking, it won't be your imagination. The late-day sun warms the miles and miles of wild blackberry bushes, and the aroma is absolutely intoxicating.

There is a huge open field for dogs to run off leash. There is a covered gazebo for picnicking and a playground for small children at the west end of the park. There are occasional benches along the riverside, but this is a nature park. It isn't manicured or manufactured. The enjoyment of being at Minto-Brown comes from observing the variety of flora, fauna, and wildlife that changes from season to season. In the winter there are flocks of sparrows. In the spring you see eagles, osprey, and hawks building their nests and fat-bellied robins gorging themselves on worms. Great Blue Heron stand as sentinels in quiet ponds and streams, almost indistinguishable from the tree snags in the water. And in the fall, the Canada Geese return by the hundreds to feed on crops the farmers have left uncut for the express purpose of providing food and shelter for wildlife.

Thanks to the efforts of 750 volunteers a few years ago, 5,000 native plants were planted to create a 200-foot buffer along sloughs and river banks. The buffer filters chemicals and helps prevent soil erosion, and provide more habitat for wildlife.

Once you begin to discover the peace and beauty of this special place, you will want to return again and again.

Ray and Joan Kroc Corps Community Center

Thanks to the herculean effort of The Salvation Army, the City of Salem and a determined group of more than 250 community leaders, Salem celebrated the Grand Opening of The Ray and Joan Kroc Corps Community Center in the fall of 2009. Located at 1865 Bill Frey Drive in northwest Salem, the 92,000-square-foot facility includes an aquatic center, a gymnasium, a dance studio, a 300-seat chapel/theater, a computer lab, meeting rooms, and a commercial kitchen.

From the beginning, the Salvation Army's goal has been to create a welcoming place for families, as well as at-risk youths. The Kroc Center serves the entire community with programs in the areas of aquatics, sports, fitness, theatre, dance, and music. The after-school and summer camp programs for kids K-12 are designed to give children from all economic levels the opportunity to enjoy interesting, exciting, and fun activities in a state-of-the-art facility.

The aquatic center features a Myrtha Technology competition pool for lap swimming, swim meets, and water polo; and it is deep enough for scuba diving certifications. The leisure pool is a favorite with a water slide that looks like a lighthouse, and a "whale tail" that spouts water. There is also a hot tub, a lazy river, and an outdoor splash pad.

Kids love coming to the center where they can choose between swimming, rock climbing, hanging out in the game room or working in the computer lab. They can enjoy some quiet reading time, or get a little tutoring help with their homework. Kids interested in physical fitness can participate in Teen Aerobics, Teens on Weights, and Teen Gladiator classes. And those who want to explore the arts can choose from programs ranging from art, to music, to theatre.

Salem's Kroc Center was funded by a gift from McDonald's heiress Joan Kroc, who left a $1.5 billion gift to The Salvation Army to build and help operate corps community centers across the country. It was a competitive process that took 20 months. After three competitive phases, The Salvation Army in Salem was awarded $35.5 million from the Ray and Joan Kroc gift to build the Community Center and $35.5 million for an endowment to help operate the facility. Local fundraising efforts brought the total contribution to $81 million.

Riverfront Park

Once an industrial site and a visual blight on the edge of downtown Salem, Riverfront Park is now a favorite play place for children and families. Located on 23 acres right next to the Willamette River, the park offers some of the most unique entertainment and artistic venues you will find anywhere.

Minto Brown Island Park in morning

Early autumn at Salem's Riverfront Park

Using Urban Renewal Funds, the property was purchased from Boise Cascade in the 1980's. People were delighted with its open grassy fields, the amphitheater, and the wide, paved walking and biking trails when the park opened in 1996.

Playground- Recognizing that children needed a place to climb and play, more than 400 members from five different Salem Rotary Clubs got involved in improving the park by raising $125,000 to build a fabulous playground that was completed in 1998.

Willamette Queen Sternwheeler- Built in Newport, Oregon in 1990, the *Willamette Queen* Sternwheeler was designed to look like the territory riverboats that once traveled the great Mississippi River. It is an 87-foot, 86-ton twin paddle wheeler that takes people out on the Willamette River for lunch and dinner excursions. Imagine – a full bar, a solid-oak dance floor, a moonlit night, and the slow, steady rhythm of the water passing over the paddle wheels. Lovely!

A.C. Gilbert's Discovery Village- A.C. Gilbert was born in Salem in 1884. He graduated from Yale with a degree in medicine. He was an Olympic gold medal winner in the pole vault, and a man whose passion was inventing toys that taught children about science, engineering, chemistry, and technology while they were happily engaged in play. The private nonprofit children's museum named for Mr. Gilbert was founded in 1989, and is located at the north end of Riverfront Park.

Now, fast forward nine years. What would you do if you had 20 miles of lumber and two tons of nails? In 1998 more than 6,000 people showed up and volunteered their time over the course of 19 days to build one of the finest outdoor children's discovery centers in the Northwest—the A.C. Gilbert's Discovery Village Backyard.

In recognition of Mr. Gilbert's most famous invention, the Erector Set, which was introduced in 1913, the main attraction of the backyard playground is the world's largest erector set tower. At 52 feet high, it provides plenty of squeals of delight and discovery as kids negotiate a path through the maze to find one of the three giant slides. Children also love playing the marimbas on the musical ensemble deck, exploring the inside of an animal cell, and testing their game-playing skills or watching a drama unfold in the Global Amphitheater.

The Gilbert House, which was built in 1887 on its current riverfront site, belonged to A.C. Gilbert's uncle. Each of the five buildings in the Village has an interesting history, but the thing that children love the most about coming to this museum is the freedom to explore and play with the interactive exhibits, including Body Basics, the Bubble Room, Dinostories, and Go Figure. Kids can touch, smell, handle, twist, and examine everything in every display. What could be more fun than that!

Salem's Riverfront Carousel- The second Old-World-style carousel to be built in the United States since the Great Depression, Salem's Riverfront Carousel, completed in the spring of 2001, stands as a testament to community spirit and cooperation.

Money for the project was raised by offering the horses for "adoption." Each horse was designed to reflect elements unique and special to the family or organization adopting it. A sketch of each design became a blueprint for the volunteer carvers.

Each horse required about 120-board feet of basswood, a pliant, hardy carving wood from a Linden tree. It took teams of 10 to 15 volunteers about 700 hours to carve the head, body, tail, and legs of each horse.

After a horse was assembled, using dowels, glue, and clamps, another group of volunteers spent an average of 50 hours sanding the seams and surface of each horse until it was baby-bottom smooth.

Finally, the horses were ready for color. Each horse was painted with an oil-based primer and then sanded. This step was repeated three times. Once the surface was prepared, layers and layers of glazes, oil paints, and enamels were added to give dimension, shading, and soft textures. Sometimes it would require up to a month for the paints to completely dry between coats.

It took five years and the dedicated efforts of hundreds of volunteers to carve and paint the horses, plan and construct the building, and raise the $1.2 million in grants and donations to make it all happen. And as wonderful as it is to hear the delighted squeals of children and watch their eyes widen as they take off on a circular flight on their favorite horse, anyone who was involved in the project will tell you that possibly the best part of Salem's Riverfront Carousel was being involved in its creation.

Eco Earth Globe- Originally an ugly black acid ball used by Boise Cascade to "cook" wood chips into pulp in the plywood mill process, it was transformed by local artists and students into a huge world globe. It took five years to create and install the 86,000 individual tiles and icons that depict the world's diversity on land and sea. A must see, the Eco Earth Globe stands today as a park favorite of children from nine to ninety-nine.

Rotary Pavilion- In April 2005, the Salem Downtown Rotary Club celebrated the completion of its One-Hundred Year Centennial Project, a 42 x 42-foot timber frame pavilion. This was not a simple project. The design featured a full-gable scissors truss, which made the structure incredibly complicated to build. Upon deciding to use Old-World style construction, which meant that notching and gravity would be used to hold the timbers together rather than nails or bolts, Rotary members realized they needed technical advice. They contacted the Timber Framers Guild, an international organization based in New Hampshire. The Guild spread the word to their membership, and more than 50 timber framers from all over the world signed on to help. They paid their own way to come to Salem to participate in this unique building project.

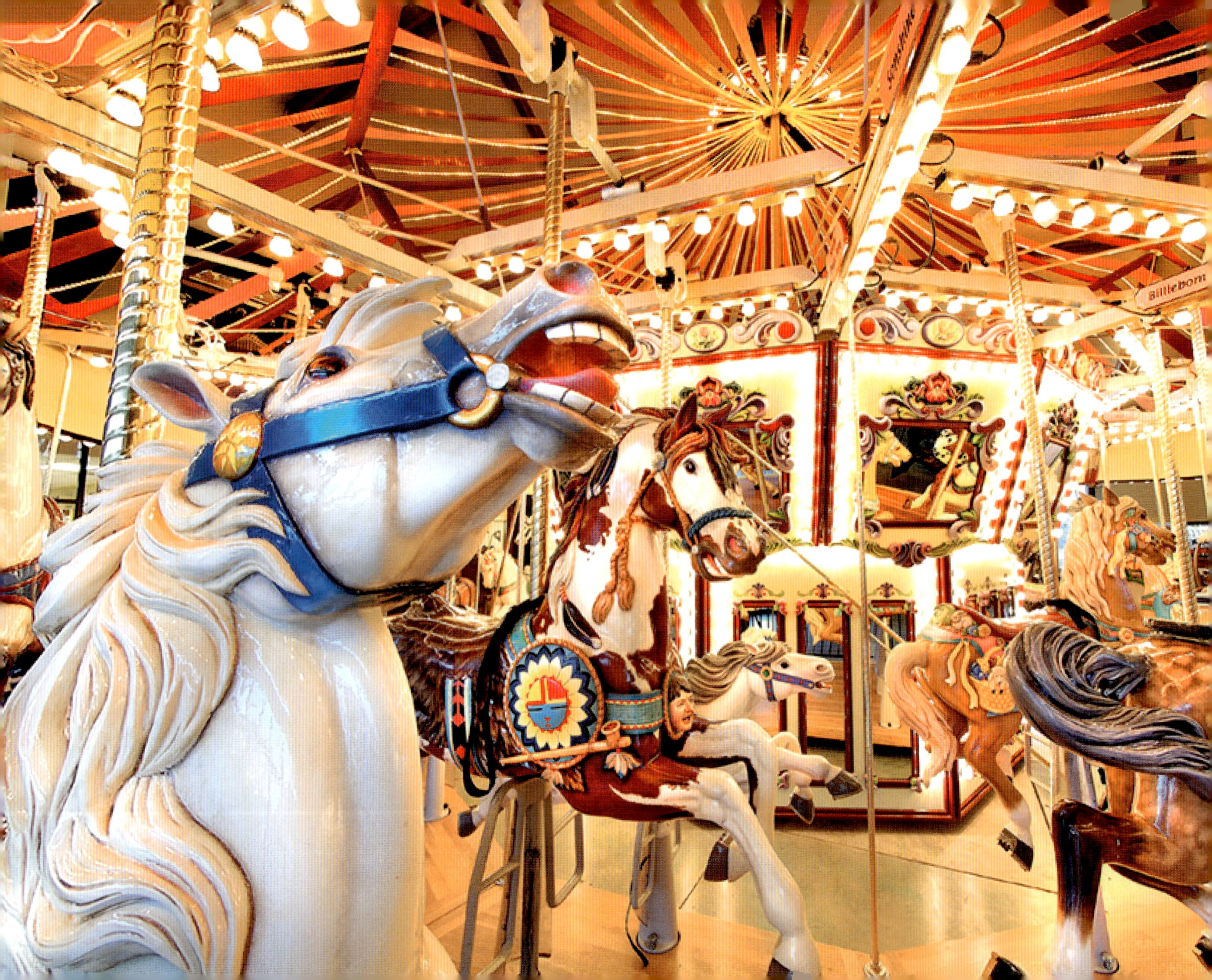

A.C. Gilbert's Discovery Village

Opposite: Salem's Riverfront Carousel

Money from an Oregon Community Foundation grant and donations from more than 100 local businesses provided the funds to purchase the timbers and other building materials. During the three weeks it took the volunteers to build the pavilion, Rotary members housed the workers and local restaurants donated meals to feed them.

Valued at just under $500,000, the Rotary Club gifted the timber, brick, and copper pavilion to the City of Salem. Capable of accommodating up to 200 people, the City rents the pavilion to groups who want to use it for picnics, gatherings, and other special events.

Asher Anderson Splash Fountain- Opened in the summer of 2009, this wonderful splash fountain was donated to the City by local philanthropist Larry Torkarski in memory of Asher Anderson, the son of good friends, who died just a few weeks after he was born.

Union Street Railroad Pedestrian Bridge- In 2004 if someone had said to you, "I have a railroad bridge I'd like to sell to you for one dollar," what do you think you might have said? The City of Salem said, "We'll buy it!" The Union Street Railroad pedestrian bridge, originally built in 1912-13, provided a badly needed connection to the communities on the east side of the Willamette to the people on the west side. Prior to that, the only way to get from one side to the other was by boat. For decades the railroad bridge linked the two communities together by transporting people and products from one side to the other. The increased use of automobiles, and the addition of the Marion Street Bridge in 1954, greatly diminished the need for a passenger train. The last train crossed the bridge in the early 1990's.

The City of Salem purchased the bridge in 2004, and it was put on the National Register of Historic Places two years later. Funding to convert it into a public walking and biking path came from a Federal Transportation Grant, The City of Salem, the Urban Renewal Agency, Oregon Department of Transportation, Oregon State Parks, Cycle Oregon, and a number of private donations.

Hundreds of people gathered in April 2009 to celebrate the grand opening of the bridge, and they followed the National Guard Band as it marched from Salem's Riverfront Park on the east bank of the Willamette to Wallace Marine Park in west Salem. The half-mile walk takes you under a 722-foot span of steel beams that look a lot like an erector set, and then you pass over a shaded, gently curving timber trestle for another 850 feet.

When out for a stroll, take the time to stop and observe the river. You are likely to see a variety of birds, the *Willamette Queen* Sternwheeler, rowing teams from Willamette University, fishermen in trolling boats, jet skiers, and speed boats passing beneath the bridge. You might even see a float plane landing or taking off.

Union Street Railroad pedestrian bridge

The Eco Earth Globe at Riverfront Park

Salem's Riverfront Park Amphitheatre-Outdoor Movie

Willamette Queen Sternwheeler

Capitol Fountain fun

A great place to shop – the Saturday Farmer's Market

Local Produce, our specialty — Wednesday Farmer's Market

Keizer Iris Festival at Schreiner's Iris Garden

South of Bethel Heights, the valley scenery is stunning

Summer fun — the Salem Art Fair & Festival

All kids invited, the Children's Parade at Salem Art Fair & Festival

After the show, the place to go — Gerry Frank's Konditorei

Downtown Salem's First Wednesday Event

Where friends meet to eat – Historic Downtown Salem

Architecturally astounding – The famous Ladd and Bush bank building

Salem Golf Club and Rudy's Restaurant

Opposite: Brilliant border, the gardens at Historic Deepwood Estate

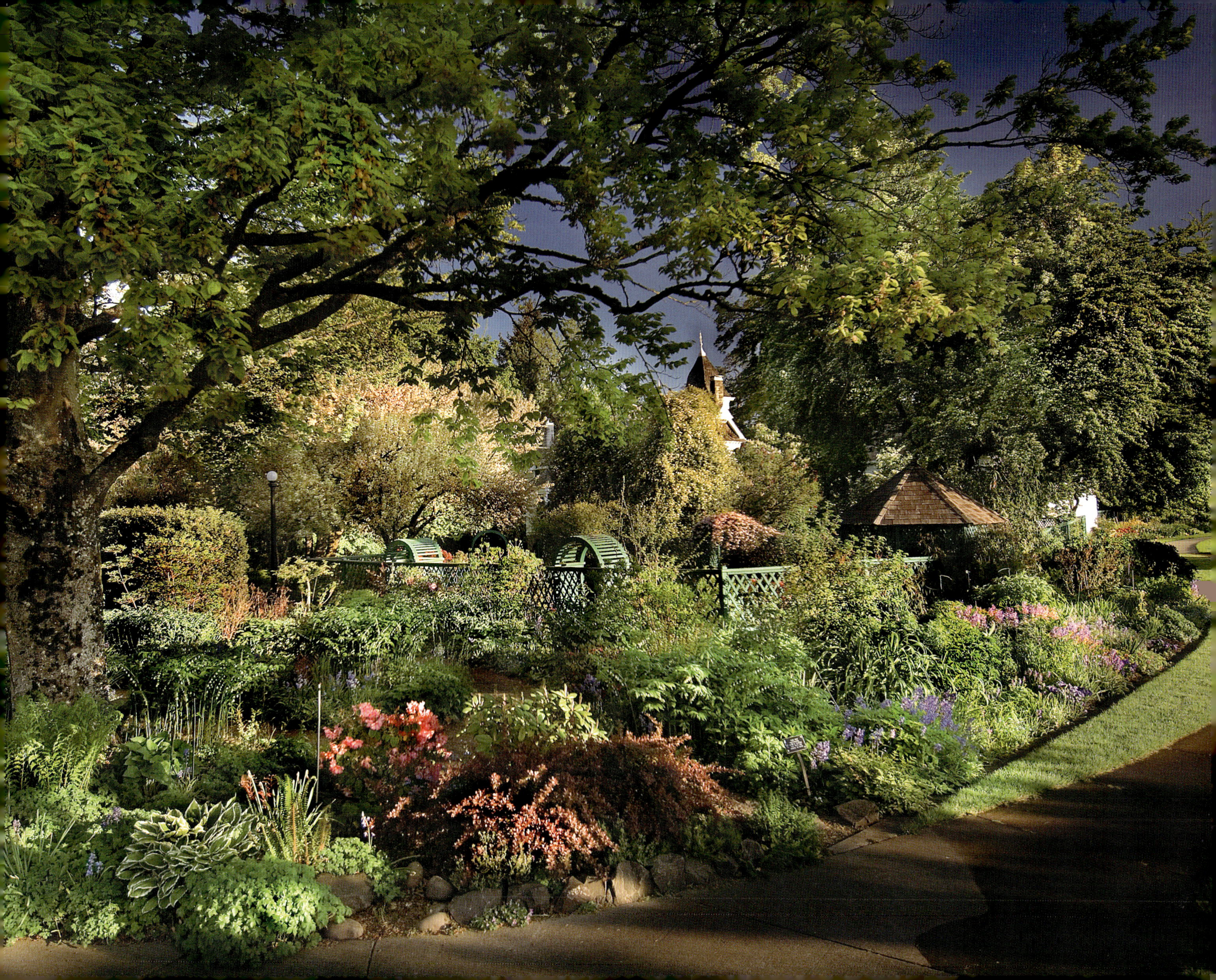

A volunteer committee called Friends of Two Bridges worked with the Mayor, the City Council and staff, and a number of state and federal agencies to make this bridge a reality. All of these groups are now engaged in trying to add another bridge that will connect Minto-Brown Park to Riverfront Park, which will ultimately make it possible for a person to walk or bike from south Salem to downtown, and on to west Salem without ever having to get on a street or cross an intersection.

Wallace Marine Park- Wallace Marine Park, considered by many to be the "Softball Capital of the Pacific Northwest," got its start when Paul Black Wallace left 24 acres of his west Salem riverfront property to the City. Subsequent purchases and gifts increased the size to 68 acres. Boat ramps and picnic facilities built in the late 1950's were swept away in the Christmas flood of 1964.

There are now five lighted softball fields and two soccer fields, which bring ball players and their families from all over the country to Salem for tournaments.

The park is now connected to Riverfront Park on the east side of the Willamette by the Union Street pedestrian bridge that opened in 2009.

Events

January through December

First Wednesday Downtown- There's a party the first Wednesday of every month in Salem, and the entire community is invited. Music, art, shopping, food and wine, along with other special activities are scheduled between 5:00 and 8:00 p.m. Friends gather and stroll the streets going in and out of various boutiques, galleries, and shops. Each First Wednesday has a theme. "Dogs Night Out" is a perennial favorite. You'll see everything from Chihuahuas in baby strollers to Great Danes wearing jewel-encrusted collars. Great fun!

April

Salem Film Festival- Salem's first film festival in 2006 was a three-day event. The community was so enthusiastic about seeing high-quality independent films and having the opportunity to visit with film makers, that the festival has now expanded to ten days. Many of the films are shown in the glitzy new Salem Cinema, a locally owned theater that specializes in presenting art, foreign, independent, and exceptional films.

Wooden Shoe Tulip Festival- Exquisite! Gorgeous! Amazing! Those are just a few of the exclamations you hear as people stroll through the 40 acres of daffodils and tulips at the Wooden Shoe Tulip Festival. Oregonians know that spring has arrived when the tulips just a few miles east of Woodburn start to bloom. The colors are outrageous, and set against a backdrop of the snow-covered Mt. Hood, it's just too pretty for words.

Bring your camera or your canvas, but be aware that the best way to appreciate the beauty and celebrate this passage out of winter may be to just take your time and soak it up as you amble through the fields and display gardens.

There are tram rides, daily entertainment events, food vendors, a market place where you can buy fresh cut flowers, gifts, and order bulbs for your garden. Kids like the cow train and setting little rubber ducks afloat in a trough as they pull the handle on an old-fashioned water pump.

May

Awesome 3000- The Awesome 3000 is recognized as one of the largest, timed, youth-only runs in the nation. It began as a fundraiser in 1983 by the Salem Schools Foundation to help save a local school. Now more than 3,000 elementary and middle-school children, including special-needs kids, participate each year. The event continues to raise money for innovative programs in local schools, but some would say that the experience of bringing the students, teachers, and community together is as rewarding as the money that is raised.

Keizer Iris Festival- The city of Keizer is located on the north edge of Salem, and it is the self-proclaimed "Iris Capital of the World." Keizer celebrates the blooming of the Iris the entire month of May, but there are four days of concentrated activity when the community gets serious about having a good time. They celebrate with carnival rides, music and dancing, food booths, arts and crafts, running and walking competitions, a golf tournament, and to top it all off, the Iris Festival Parade.

At the center of this celebration is the Schreiner's Iris Gardens, the nation's largest retail grower of Iris. During the spring bloom season, thousands of Iris, from the deepest black-purple to the purest white (and every color in between) bloom on the 200 acres of flower fields surrounding a manicured ten-acre display garden. The fields and display garden are open for viewing every day from dawn to dusk and you can see for yourself what can be accomplished when a family dedicates seventy-five years to breeding and growing the finest Iris in the world.

Historic Deepwood Estate – Winter wonderland

The tranquil grounds of the Mt. Angel Abbey, 17 miles north of Salem

For many people, packing a lunch or dinner to enjoy while sitting at a picnic table overlooking the garden is a spring tradition. It also presents a perfect opportunity to take home an extravagant bouquet (very reasonably priced) or order bulbs for your own garden.

May & November

Weekend Wine Tasting Events- Wine Country Memorial Day & Wine Country Thanksgiving. The weekends of Memorial Day and Thanksgiving are extra special for wine lovers in the Mid-Willamette Valley. More than 100 wineries open their doors to the public for barrel tastings and samplings of new releases. Many wineries are only open to the public these two weekends each year, so it's good to do a little research ahead of time to help you decide how to best spend your time.

You could choose to visit just one winery where you could take the time to have a leisurely conversation with the owner and winemaker while tasting their offerings. You could visit three or four wineries each day so you could taste and compare some of the best the Valley has to offer. Or you could gather up a group of friends and hire a limousine or a bus to take you from one winery to another in search of the perfect Pinot Noir.

Some winery tastings are free, others charge. Some enhance the ambiance and pleasure by offering food and music. If you're lucky and the weather cooperates, you might get to sit outside and soak up a few rays of sun while enjoying the beauty of the countryside.

May through October

Farmer's Market- Buy Fresh – Buy Local is the theme of the Farmer's Market held every Wednesday and Saturday, May through October. Over 300 vendors offer everything from organic produce to fresh baked bread, from handmade soaps and cheese to beaded jewelry and exquisite bouquets of flowers. There is music and live entertainment and fresh, delicious food prepared on site – all grown, created, and baked by the vendor selling it. Free parking, no admission – just great local produce and products offered in a festival atmosphere.

June

Soap Box Derby- Salem's Soap Box Derby has been drawing youths, ages 8-17 for nearly 60 years. The "Build Your Own Racer" championship event in June is a one-day, winner-take-all race, with the winner in each division earning the right to compete in Akron, Ohio for the World Championship title. A number of Salem winners have gone on to win that prestigious title.

World Beat Festival- In 2009 Salem's World Beat Festival won the Ovation Award for best festival or event in Oregon from the Oregon Festival and Events Association. It is a two-day celebration of international music, dance, food, folklore, and hands-on crafts celebrating the people of every continent and their traditions. Salem's Riverfront Park swells with people who come to watch the costumed processions, performances, demonstrations, and workshops. Each of the five World Villages includes a children's area offering free, hands-on cultural crafts. The Festival is conducted by the Salem Multicultural Institute, a nonprofit, volunteer organization dedicated to promoting harmony and understanding through innovative, educational and cultural programs and activities.

July

Fourth of July Fireworks- Music, food, and fireworks over the Willamette at dusk bring friends and families together at Salem's Riverfront Park for an old-fashioned hometown Independence Day Celebration.

Salem Art Fair and Festival- People in Salem plan their summer vacations around the third weekend in July. You just don't want to be out of town during the Salem Art Fair and Festival. It's a 60-year plus tradition that offers three days of art, music, food, and fun under the canopy of Bush Park's historic oak trees.

Ask any of the 200 top artists and craftspeople who come from across the U.S. and Canada, and they will tell you that the Salem Art Fair is one of the most enjoyable and profitable shows they will participate in all year.

If you ask some of the 100,000 or so people who attend each year what they like the most, you might get answers like:

- The art is fabulous!
- The food is delicious!
- The Kids Court is fun!
- The music by regional and national performers is wonderful!
- The micro-brew beer is cold, and the Northwest wines are exquisite!

The Art Fair is the major fundraiser for the Salem Art Association, which at nearly 90 years, is one of the largest, oldest and most comprehensive art organizations in the Northwest.

The money raised from this event, helps support artists in the community, as well as more than 10,000 children, teachers, and parents in the surrounding area through its In School Community Arts Education Program, which includes classes, workshops, and camps.

World Beat Festival Dancers

Dragon Boat races on the Willamette River

Willamette Valley Vineyards south of Salem

August - September

Oregon State Fair- Every year since 1862, people have flocked to Salem in late summer to attend the Oregon State Fair. Touted as being "Too Big to Miss" the fair offers eleven days of entertainment, exhibits, displays and competitions. Farm animals, home arts, fine arts, photography, gardening, science and technology are all accessible.

Artists and craftspeople demonstrate their techniques and show off their skills; and families flock to the Familyville stage for free daily performances and shows. From scuba diving, to rock climbing, to rock stars, equestrian events, concerts, and carnival rides, you can experience old-fashioned fun while participating in new-age technology.

You can visit with Oregon authors, buy a myriad of products from commercial vendors, and if you want to participate in a totally unique and fairly exclusive event, you can attend the only all-Oregon Wine Competition and Awards Ceremony in the beautiful Hart of the Garden. Approximately 50 wineries and a dozen Oregon chefs hand out samples of their best creations and compete for Best in Show.

September

Willamette Valley Vineyards Grape Stomping Championship and Harvest Celebration- Willamette Valley Vineyards, a local winery that sits high atop a hill just a few miles south of Salem and offers views worthy of a travel poster, hosts this squishy, squashy, stomping event every year to celebrate the successful conclusion of the grape harvest. Teams of two, a stomper and a swabber, crush grapes between their toes. The team that produces the most juice wins a trip to the World Grape Stomping Championship in Santa Rosa, California.

Hint - If you're not into stomping, you can be a spectator. You can dance and eat barbeque, and you can even slip into the tasting room, or amble out onto the deck overlooking the gorgeous Willamette Valley and sample some of the winery's elegant, classic, award-winning wines.

Mt. Angel Oktoberfest- A small community settled by German pioneers in the 1800's, Mt. Angel established the Oktoberfest in 1966 in celebration of the bounty of the earth and the goodness of creation. It has grown into Oregon's largest folk festival. More than 30 musical groups perform continuous live music on four stages. There's dancing in the streets on Friday and Saturday nights.

You will find the traditional Biergarten, Weingarten, and Alpinegarten, a large arts and crafts show, and more than 50 vendors offering enticing varieties of ethnic foods. If you plan to spend the night, there is ample room for RV's and tents.

December

Thousands of Salem residents kick off their holiday festivities by attending the Tree Lighting in Riverfront Park followed by the PGE Festival of Lights Holiday Parade, the largest nighttime illuminated holiday parade west of the Mississippi! A large section of downtown Salem is closed to traffic so residents can line the sidewalks, sip hot chocolate, and sometimes huddle under umbrellas as they watch the variety of illuminated floats, vehicles, pets, and bands pass in review.

Salem is the place

Often referred to as "The Land of Plenty," this is a place where opportunities abound. If you're looking for a good time, you will certainly find a world of entertainment options starting in the mountains, sweeping through the Valley, and going all the way to the Pacific Ocean. And…Travel Salem can assist you with all your touring needs, www.TravelSalem.com

If you are an entrepreneur, you will find that this is a business-friendly city. With an outstanding city government, a great Chamber of Commerce, and SEDCOR, Salem's Strategic Economic Development Corporation, and there are people who will do whatever it takes to help you succeed.

And if you are a person who likes to be involved, you will find that the opportunities to serve and contribute in a meaningful way are nearly limitless.

Come spend a little time with us. But beware, once you discover all Salem and the surrounding area has to offer, you may never want to leave.

Kids love the Witch's Head

Fun for all – Enchanted Forest Theme Park

Salem Keizer Volcanoes baseball, and their delightful mascot "Crater" (Courtesy of Salem Keizer Volcanoes)

About the Author

Elaine K. Sanchez is an author and professional speaker who is passionate about helping others find hope and humor in aging, illness, and long-term caregiving. She is a member of the National Speakers Association, and travels throughout the country talking to groups about getting prepared to care for family elders and surviving the emotional stress of caregiving.

Her keynotes and workshops are based on her book, *Letters from Madelyn*, *Chronicles of a Caregiver*, a tender, gritty, and uproariously funny story about life, love, and long-term caregiving.

Elaine grew up on a Kansas dairy farm. She earned her living as a sales manager for network television affiliates in Colorado and New Mexico. She served on numerous nonprofit and professional boards, including the Marketing Advisory Group for the NBC Television Network.

Upon moving to Salem in 1998, she retired from the broadcast industry and immediately got involved in her new community. She wrote two children's books for Salem's Riverfront Carousel, *How Francis Got His Wink*, and *The General's Secret*. In 2006, she co-founded Salem's first film festival.

She is married to Alex Sanchez, a professor at Oregon State University. Together they have eight children, eight grandchildren, and a full and happy life.

About the Photographer

Ron Cooper is a self-taught photographer whose name is familiar to readers of the *Oregon Statesman* and *Statesman Journal* newspapers from the 1970's through his retirement in 2000.

In 1969, Ron moved his family to Salem to continue his career in photojournalism. During his tenure at the newspaper, he covered two national presidential nominating conventions and had two assignments in the now-former Soviet Union. His photography has won numerous national awards, and much local appreciation. His photos of volunteers and the carousel horses they carved formed the basis of a book on the Salem Riverfront Carousel.

Photo by Cathy Pozar

His wife, Penny, was an elementary school teacher in Salem for almost 30 years, and died of cancer in 2000. Visitors to the Salem Hospital now enjoy many of Ron's photos, which he donated in honor of Penny's memory. Ron remains an active member of the Salem community. In addition to continuing his photography, he plays music at local nursing homes, an activity that he has enjoyed for 20 years.

Cooper's interest in photography only intensified after his retirement. He has traveled extensively and trained his lens on people and places around the U.S. and abroad, but continues to photograph the subject that he knows best— Salem, and the Mid-Willamette Valley. This passion and dedication has enabled him to amass one of the most comprehensive collections of Salem photographs of the past decade. Check out his web site at www.roncooperphotography.com.

"I was a history major, not a journalism major, and I especially enjoy photographing Salem's many historical sites. The photographs I leave of this beautiful city and region will be my legacy to the future."

Mahonia Hall, home and official residence of Oregon's Governor

Rear Cover: Beautiful Poppy Valley from south Salem hills